Damn Death Did Us Part

PALMETTO
PUBLISHING
Charleston, SC
www.PalmettoPublishing.com

© 2024 by Kenna Narducci

All rights reserved.
This book or any portion thereof may not be reproduced or used in any manner whatsoever without the express written permission of the publisher except for the use of brief quotations in a book review.

Paperback ISBN: 979-8-8229-4019-2

Damn Death Did Us Part

I WENT TO WORK A WIFE
AND CAME HOME A WIDOW

KENNA NARDUCCI

For those that love me at my worst and encourage me at my weakest.

For the person I was when I started writing this book and the person I am now.

Thank you.

Sharing My Story

I originally started writing for myself. It was a way to say all the words that I wanted to say, I guess, without saying them. I did not write with the intention of sharing all these personal thoughts and feelings with the world. What I have come to realize recently is how strong I am. If I, with my words, can inspire one person to weather the storm ahead, I think overcoming my vulnerability is worth it.

I have always worried about offending or disappointing those close to me. I just want to "do right" and make them proud. Well, can I let you in on a little secret? If you are an adult, you cannot get in trouble with another adult if you are not breaking a law.

People are always going to judge and have their own opinions on how others should live their lives and the choices others make. You are not tequila or tacos; you cannot make everyone happy. At the end of the day, your happiness is the most important, and those who truly support you will always be there.

So here is my dirty laundry, my empty wine bottles, and the nights when we had dessert for dinner. The story of the good, the bad, the beautiful, and the ugly. A raw look into the emotional life of a widow, with tips and guidance on navigating the grief, confusion, and desolation. I've written my journey with no filter (on my words—I plead the fifth on my pictures).

This is my story, these are my feelings, and this is unapologetically me.

Chapter 1
THE DAY I BECAME THE W-WORD.

I want to start this chapter out by reminding everyone *hard is hard.* I am not here to say my loss is greater or more significant than someone else's. I am just giving you my story; I have found that owning my story is part of my healing process. Loss is what connects us, grief is what guides us, and love is what saves us.

Picture 2020 in the state of California, which shut salons down for months. I have turned into a second-grade teacher for my son and a housewife with the worry of having no income. I finally get to go back to work at the end of May. On June 17 I was in the middle of a haircut when I get the phone call that my husband has had a heart attack and the paramedics are on their way. That one phone call was the moment my life changed forever. For nine excruciating minutes, I drove from my salon, and then I watched my husband being wheeled on a gurney out of the house we called home. We were living in COVID times, so the paramedics informed me I couldn't ride in the ambulance. Without hesitation I jumped into my car, nearly ran over the nosiest neighbor who was trying to stop me, and followed the ambulance, making phone calls to my in-laws, my mom, my best friend, and my husband's friend.

I parked in the emergency room parking lot, and as I was walking to the entrance, I locked eyes with one of the paramedics who'd brought Greg in, and I knew it wasn't good. The nurse handed me a mask and asked me to wait outside while they figured out his status. Out walked a man identifying himself as the hospital's chaplain, asking me to follow him to a private room. He explained to me that they were still working on my husband, and he was trying to find out if I could be by Greg's side (remember, we were in the middle of a pandemic). He left and came back shortly, letting me know that the doctor had given me permission to be with him, but it would be intense and there would be many people in the room.

The vision that has stuck with me the most is that of watching two gentlemen switch off standing on a stool in full gowns, masks, and shields, giving my over-six-foot, 320-pound husband chest compressions. The sweat beaded off their foreheads, one man resting on a chair in the corner, waiting to take his position next. I choked back sobs and sang lyrics to a song Greg had written for a girlfriend that had passed away before he started dating me: "You're my angel eyes; I'll see you on the other side; I will be waiting." Looking back, yes, I think it's weird that out of all the songs in the world, that's the one that came to mind…but maybe part of me hopes that's what he would have been saying to me at that moment. I am forever grateful for the compassion the doctors and nurses showed me—they explained everything they were doing, and their eyes showed me sorrow and sympathy.

I prayed while holding his hand, but it wasn't the warm hand I'd held the day before; it was cold and starting to turn purple…I knew he was gone. The words came out of my mouth: "We're done…he's gone." The doctors and nurses funneled out of the room, leaving just me, the chaplain, and the shell of my husband. The chaplain asked if I wanted some time alone with Greg. I declined but asked if he would pray over him.

As I walked out of that ER to meet my husband's friend Jason and my mom, it was like the world was racing around me and I was in slow mode. I will never forget the look on Jason's face as he looked at me, and I broke down crying in his big bear hug. I guess I knew that could be my moment of weakness before I had to go home and tell our son that his best friend and idol was now his guardian angel.

The drive home was blurry, but I recall the stop sign I was at as I heard my mother-in-law's heart break when I told his family he didn't make it. I also remember the 7-Eleven I passed when I told my best friend, "He didn't make it." The overpass I was on when my sister answered the phone and I blurted out in sobs, "He's gone—Greg's dead." Next thing I knew, I was sitting in the car in front of my house, looking at my mascara-stained cheeks in the mirror. My son, Cash, was in the house with our good friends Arthur and Nikki and their two children, Rhys and Brooklynn.

I moved from the front door to the bathroom as fast as I could, then turned on the water to wash my face and take a deep breath. Greg's dirty clothes were scattered on the floor of the bathroom. Under my breath I said, "Of course you would, asshole." He was notorious for leaving his dirty clothes on the floor; why not have that be one of the last things he did?

Here went nothing...I walked out of the bathroom, made eye contact with Arthur and Nikki, and gave them a quick shake of the head. Then I asked Cash to come out back with me. It was there the entire neighborhood heard the cries of an eight-year-old: "*No*! But I called 911!" He then let out gut-wrenching sobs because he had just lost the most important man in his life. This precious boy was no stranger to death, you see—it was exactly one year and one month to the day his Pops went to heaven—but this was different. We were able to have our goodbyes with Pops; Cash didn't get that with his dad.

It was at this moment I watched my best friend, who was only a few days post hysterectomy and supposed to be in bed, slowly move across my living room to give me a hug. One of my mom's dear friends who is a chaplain had arrived before my mom even made it to the house from the hospital. My sister showed up with a big bag of mostly dirty clothes only to realize the next day she had no underwear, no socks, and no toothbrush. Let's not forget the nosy neighbor, Crazy Carol, trying to invite herself in. My house was so busy with people yet felt so empty at the same time.

Not even an hour after I broke the news to my child, I was alerted by my sister that a friend of my husband's had decided to post about his death on social media.

While I know he didn't intentionally try to hurt anyone, it felt so callous. We hadn't even told all our family...

I formulated a post and picked a couple of pictures, feeling like this was it, my first goodbye to him, and I didn't even get the opportunity to have the "proper" amount of time to write it. Really, who was I kidding? Would any amount of time feel proper? I was thirty-four and had just become a widow, and now I was announcing it to the world.

Chapter 2
EULOGY

Initially, I didn't plan on including this in the book, but let's face it…attempting to summarize the love you have for the person you thought you were spending the rest of your life within a single speech is damn near impossible. If you find yourself struggling to put your feelings into words, hell, borrow mine. Straight up copy and paste…your crowd may give you some funny looks, but it might be worth the laugh.

***

Thank you for being here today. The love and support our family has received shows what a remarkable impact Greg had on everyone.

I know Greg is looking down right now, and I truly believe he knows just how loved he really was…In fact, I wouldn't be surprised if he and Tom have placed bets as to how many people would show up today, and Greg is basking in all the attention. He had a larger-than-life personality, a heart that wanted to help everyone, and an endless list of talents.

From a young age, Greg knew how to captivate an audience. Whether he was drumming on his brother's vinyl records, doing the moonwalk at a wedding, or selling golf balls that he'd just cleaned up after diving for them in golf course ponds, everyone knew who he was. He always knew which friends' houses had the best snacks; you could always entice him with some good food. Greg had a way of making something that was his idea seem like it was yours, and before you knew it, you were agreeing to something you originally didn't want to do. When he was twenty-five, he caught my attention on-stage. He claims I stalked him, but I'd have to say the stalking was mutual. Over the years I found myself telling Greg to quit making new friends; we couldn't keep up with the ones we had…That didn't stop him; he never met a stranger.

Greg was known as the "cool dad" that drove the tow truck and never hesitated when one of the kids wanted to see how the controls worked. Then came his role as football coach; his beard embodied our mascot, the Viking, and he wore his Viking horns with pride. Greg had a way of making the most discouraged players smile, all while cracking jokes with the other coaches. His impact on those he encountered will remain in our hearts forever.

Greg was always there to help a friend in need. Want to learn how to ride a dirt bike? Call Greg. Need hunting or fishing tips? Call Greg. Get your truck stuck in an orchard? Call Greg. Does your son need the birds-and-bees talk? Call Greg—only to find out that conversation didn't go quite according to plan. Put the wrong size shell in your shotgun? Call Greg. Need a piece of furniture moved? Call Greg. Need your car fixed? Call Greg. Need a cookie taste tester— or let's be honest, any food tested? Call Greg. Need a good laugh? Call Greg. He was always there, just as long as it wasn't through text message; he hated texting.

Greg's hobbies were plentiful; whether it was music, working on cars, riding dirt bikes, hunting, fishing, or football, he always joked that he didn't understand why people would ever spend money on drugs or alcohol when there are so many other cool things you could spend your money on. The funny thing is, he was good at all of it…but you know what happens when you have a son? That's expensive hobbies times two. Watching his latest music project, Greedy Lion, flourish the last couple of years was like watching his soul light on fire. You see, he stepped away from the music scene shortly after becoming a father because he didn't want to miss out on being a dad. He wanted to be present; he wanted to mold this precious little boy into something incredible.

Cash became his father's shadow, naturally picking up his charisma and becoming his mini-me and partner in crime. You should have seen the two of them use zip ties and belts to make a pair of waders that was three sizes too big to fit Cash just so they could go duck hunting together. Or the time they added a light bar and straight piped the go-kart so now the whole neighborhood could not only see but also hear them from a mile away. Watching Greg jump up and down on the sidelines with tears in his eyes when Cash scored his first touchdown was nothing short of magical. But the most precious moments were the evenings when Greg would crawl into Cash's bed and cuddle him until he fell asleep.

To My Love
At twenty-two I was your girlfriend.
At twenty-six I was your son's mother.
At twenty-nine I was your wife.
At thirty-four I am your widow.
You left me twelve days shy of twelve years together.
You often said that I saved you, but the truth is we saved each other.

When you told me the song "All I Need" was for me, I thought it was a little awkward that my baby brother was singing it…then I asked you to break down every verse because I didn't understand how it related to our relationship; you told me to stop overanalyzing it and take the message "All I need is you." Who knew that those verses would have more meaning as I held your hand, praying to God to give you back to me?

So today I honor you, and I promise to raise our son with faith, love, strength, humility, and laughter. It's what you did every day.

Chapter 3
EARLY DAZE

It is hard to explain the suffocating effect that grief can have on your mind, body, and spirit, especially in the early days of loss. It's being surrounded by so many people and feeling so lonely at the same time. It's wanting to be comforted, but the person you want to console you can't. It's having so much to do but knowing the one person you would rather be doing it with won't be there.

Getting the Help You Need
Nighttime was always the hardest for me; I wasn't surrounded by people, and I had to be strong for my son, who was in my bed. The first night I don't think I slept more than three hours. I would wake up and pace through the house, sobbing, looking for something, just not quite sure what that something was.

I remember my first big breakdown like it was yesterday. My dad and stepmom, who had come to stay with me from out of state, took my son for the day to go visit family. I stayed back, really needing some alone time. A friend stopped by to drop off a meal, and the sadness in his eyes cut me to the core. I set the food on the counter, thanked him with a hug, shut the front door, and fell to the kitchen floor in tears. For hours I lay there creating a puddle of tears on the cold tile. Looking back, I think this was the moment I realized he was never going to come back. I have never felt more alone in my life.

Within the first couple of days, I was at the bookstore, scouring the self-help section and looking at books about widowhood. I was dumbfounded that there weren't many books on young widowhood. I couldn't relate to most of the titles on the shelf. I needed to find support from something relatable, but this was tough to find with the looming effects of COVID restrictions. So I got on social media and joined a "Young Widows with Children" group.

It was this group that taught me that everyone grieves differently. Some people needed to sleep with their spouses' urns; me, I didn't even want the thing on my mantle. Others were asking for dating advice; I simply wasn't ready. I hadn't even washed his dirty clothes. Quite honestly, I stashed them in my nightstand and smelled them in my darkest moments, knowing that eventually the smell would dissipate with the memory of him. I don't think I lasted more than three weeks in that group. I needed more help than this group could offer me.

I am not a stranger to going to therapy; I have seen a counselor on and off most of my life. I learned many great tools over the years, but I always felt a little misunderstood. I have been spiritually sensitive most of my life but was raised to think it was not okay. I did the only thing I could and bottled these senses away…

Here's the funny thing: you can ignore spiritual gifts all you want, but they will find a way back into your life. My gifts would frequently visit in my dreams when my guard was down. So, there I was after Greg died, getting only few hours of rest a night and really not sleeping at all because my higher self was contacting me during this time. I was desperate for direction and was introduced to Eileen, a counselor who also practices clairvoyance, astrology, Reiki, and so much more…the kicker is that she herself is a widow. She has a way of guiding you to your own intuitional answers that allows you to build trust and love with yourself. Why is this important? Because after everything you have endured with loss, at the end of the day, all you have is yourself.

I remember that the first time Greg came through to Eileen in a session, he said he wanted things to be okay and he was finally able to breathe again. Now, I know some of you don't believe in things like this. I respect that, but I have found more healing in this therapy than any other form. Not only do we all grieve differently, but we also all heal differently. There isn't one answer to it all.

Let. Them. Help.
I am fighting every urge to place a clapping emoji after every word of that heading. And before you get started, I know it's hard to let people do things for you; sometimes you want the busywork so you can forget about your current situation. I can speak from experience: the time will come when the people around you return to their

day-to-day lives, and you will have to do it all on your own. This won't last forever.

I recommend having a point person or people, someone who has your best interest at heart. I was lucky to have my mom, sister, and best friend take on this role for me. My mom was the point person for contacting our family, the hospital, and funeral home. My sister and best friend organized a meal train, got people over to help around the house, canceled all my appointments at work, and dealt with visitors and gifts when I didn't want to see anyone. Take the reprieve, and when people offer, *let them.*

Journal, journal, journal…You are in such a brain fog during the early part of widowhood that half the time you can't tell whether you are coming or going. Write it down, whether it's something as simple as what day you put the load of laundry in the washer or as weighty as what time you have a meeting at the funeral home. Write about your feelings and emotions: the good, the bad, or the ugly. Pencil in a memory, whether it brought you joy or pain. Every bit of your journey is important. Thanks to all the time I spent journaling, I now have the ability to look back and appreciate my resiliency and growth… plus I get to write this badass book.

Post on social media. Sure, it might seem morbid to some people that you are still trying to live some semblance of a normal life but screw them. I walked through that first year in such a fog, really—I was just going through the motions. Sometimes, those social media memories are the only reminders of how I navigated that first year. In fact, right before our second Christmas without Greg, I couldn't have told you what we did for that first year. How sad is that? Well, social media reminded me that we ordered pizza for Christmas dinner, and what is ironic is that in our second year, we decided to make homemade pizza. I guess subconsciously I knew that pizza on Christmas was our new tradition. A tradition that we have decided to continue.

Just remember this journey is all your own. Don't be afraid to ask for help, and even more importantly, don't turn down someone who is offering to help. What works for one may not work for another. Try it all if you have to. I was one more breakdown from turning my life into an episode of *Glee*— I was just going to sing and dance everywhere in life before I ended up as a special story on *Snapped*. Luckily for everybody's sake, that didn't happen.

Chapter 4
DECANONIZATION AND COMMUNICATION

One of the most beneficial exercises my therapist had me do when my husband passed away was to decanonize him. It is natural in the grieving process to focus on the positive memories and qualities that made someone special to us; unfortunately, it can also make the magnitude of the loss feel greater. You decanonize the person by writing a list of the attributes you didn't like. This exercise isn't intended to portray the person negatively; it's meant to help you recognize the qualities or actions you don't want in your life.

I have made the bold choice to share my personal thoughts and emotions with the world, so I am sharing my list. Again, I am not sharing this to paint Greg in a bad light; his good qualities far outweighed his bad. This exercise also brought to light my own shortcomings in our marriage—*that* I wasn't prepared for.

Reasons I am happy my marriage is over:
- Less financial strain/responsibility
- House is less messy
- No pressure to cook dinner or keep a tidy house
- I can make all the decisions
- Less laundry
- No pee on the bathroom floor
- Dirty clothes are not where they shouldn't be
- I don't feel like I have two kids

Marriage is hard. Losing Greg was hard. Doing this exercise and realizing that the frustrations I experienced were a direct result of what I accepted from the beginning of our relationship: even harder.

I was, and in some cases still am, terrible at balancing. I often catch myself putting others' needs before my own. Looking back over the years, I can see it's a vicious cycle I have repeated my whole life. Either I give too much, or I don't give at all, only to reach a point of total exhaustion where I completely shut down. Well, let me tell you something…you cannot expect someone to know what your needs are if you are not communicating those needs.

Here's where the light bulb really turned on…I realized the person I had to communicate my needs to the most was myself. Isn't it funny how pointing out the flaws in someone else can hold a light to your own shortcomings? The challenges in my marriage all circled back to one thing…communication.

It is crucial from the very beginning of a relationship to establish open communication about the needs and wants for both sides. If you tolerate a certain behavior for many years, it is unrealistic to have change at the drop of a hat; have those hard conversations about expectations early on.

Cleaning. I did it all. Why? Because I never asked him to help, and, well, he never volunteered. Almost eight years into our relationship, on February 22, 2019 (I know the date thanks to documenting it via Facebook), I lost it. Like I *lost it* lost it. I handed him the bathroom cleaning supplies and told him to have at it. My avid hunting husband could hit a duck in mid-flight but couldn't aim into a stationary toilet bowl. It drove me nuts. I literally cleaned his piss for almost eight years, and he let me…because I allowed the behavior and did not communicate my frustrations earlier in the relationship.

Feel free to judge my behavior, including virtually documenting him finally cleaning the bathroom. I have had numerous individuals tell me it was trivial, and here are their excuses…

- "It's just cleaning the bathroom."
- "It's just what men do."
- "But he works long hours; he shouldn't have to clean."

Here's the thing: my frustrations were valid, because at the end of the day, *it mattered to me.* I felt like I was being taken for granted. Yes, it was just cleaning the bathroom, so why was it always my job to do it? I was raised in a home with a father and brother who *never* left pee on the floor (excuse debunked). I worked too. In fact, I paid more than 75 percent of our household bills, cooked, and kept a clean house. So many unmet expectations—all because there was no communication.

By decanonizing Greg, I was made aware of my own shortcomings, not only in our marriage but also in my relationship with myself. That is not easy to admit, because, well, I thought I was pretty damn near perfect. Now that I realize how crucial clear communication is, I have to hold myself accountable in future relationships, but most importantly with myself.

Chapter 5
IDENTITY CRISIS

There is nothing like a life-changing event to make you reevaluate and question everything. I have always been a type A personality with a plan. I had my weekly goals, six-month goals, one-year goals, five-year goals, and so on and so forth. Well, having my spouse drop dead wasn't in my timeline, and it really put a wrench in my plans.

Losing Greg had me spinning in circles internally. From the outside I looked "normal," or as normal as a new widow could be. I resumed what I could of my life (remember, this was 2020 in the middle of a pandemic, in California) and jumped back into something of a routine, and I had a lot of people convinced I was okay.

It's hard being labeled a widow. The pitiful looks you get when you randomly run into people you know. Now, I know it was not their fault that they didn't know how to respond to my current life situation, but hell, neither did I. At least offer me a shot or a damn cookie.

My home felt empty. Really, it didn't feel like a home. I tried redecorating; I bought new bedding, a new couch, a new entertainment center…still empty. My mom and sister redesigned my back patio. It was gorgeous, the only place I felt solace. I could sit outside in the glow of the lights, not realizing hours had passed as I scrolled through memories on my phone, downing a bottle of wine or a few margaritas.

While I went through the motions when I was at work, I couldn't help but flashback to that day. Getting the phone call, throwing my shears on the station and hearing them drop on the floor (go ahead, other hairdressers: I know, cringe), asking a coworker to finish my client, running out to my car without my purse, and being stuck at the awful red light for what felt like an eternity. What was once my home away from home felt like a prison of grief.

It Was Time for Change…
I want to take you back to August 2019. It was the first time I traveled to Greenville, South Carolina. It was a weeklong trip with my sister, and I absolutely fell in love with the area. It was like God told me I would need this place one day. I spent the next ten months trying to convince my husband that this was where we were meant to live. On June 15, 2020, he agreed to give it a shot and at least visit Greenville. Unfortunately, he never got to experience the beauty of the area because just two days later, he passed away suddenly from a heart attack. It was while I was driving to his viewing that James Taylor's "Carolina in My Mind" started playing through the car

stereo and I had this gut feeling that South Carolina was where I was meant to go.

Everyone says, "Don't make any big decisions in the first year." I say follow your intuition and do whatever the hell you want, as long as it doesn't bring any harm to others. I knew South Carolina was where I needed to be for my healing process. Nine months after Greg's passing, I flew to Greenville and bought a home, and three months later Cash and I moved into what would become our sanctuary.

It was a chance for a fresh start. I sold most of our belongings before the move, so everything was new. I took my time furnishing the home with things I wanted and decorating the way I wanted, because I was the grown-up and I could do what I wanted. It was my home...a safe space where I could do things in my own time without feeling the judgment of others.

The biggest benefit of the move was that I got to take an entire year off work. No pressure to prove myself to anyone but myself. I could breathe and just be a mom... an opportunity I would have felt guilty for if I'd still been in California. While I planned to take the time off, the universe taught me a very important lesson: all the planning in the world cannot force what isn't meant to be.

Getting my cosmetology license in South Carolina was not an easy feat. I had to retest, and testing dates were months and months out. I still had my teaching job, where I taught other stylists the science and technology of a hair-color brand. I had the rude awakening that the brand did not have the notoriety here on the East Coast that it did on the West Coast. Classes were few and far between, and I was growing restless. In the meantime, I was offered a job serving and bartending.

I thought, what a great way to meet people and build a clientele once I am back behind the chair. Once again, the joke would be on me...

I started my time behind the salon chair in November 2022, and by May 2023, I realized I was juggling too much. While I love the beauty industry, I didn't think I wanted to be in it in the same capacity anymore. I had come to enjoy going to work, clocking in, clocking out, and leaving work at work. I know I don't want to be a bartender forever, but for now, it's perfect for me.

I was trying to fit my old life into my new life, and the pieces were not fitting together. So I set them down. Because guess what...*I can if I want to*. My whole life, I used to think that my value was determined by the amount of money I made; I now know it's not. All that matters is that I'm happy, and the Lord will provide.

Through loss I have learned that it is okay not to have all the answers and that you are allowed to reinvent yourself to stay true to your new path. When the wave of uneasiness overwhelms you, take a step back, because it's okay not to be okay. Go ahead and roll your eyes at the statement; I have many times. Maybe, just maybe, instead of simply responding with an "I know," it's really time for us to believe it. When all else fails, give in to what God and the universe have planned for you, reinvent yourself, and stay true to your new path...and if you really are like me, loosen up with a drink and a slice of cake—it always does the trick!

Chapter 6
IT'S OKAY TO LIVE IN THE LONELY...

I never want to be viewed as weak, so I jumped into life as a widow the best way I knew how: keeping myself busy. I jumped right back into work at the salon and being a mom; I did more traveling that first year than I had in years. From the outside I looked like I had it all together. So many people complimented my ability to handle everything that had happened. Truth was, I was desperately lonely and craving the support of a significant other.

Dating
This is the part of my story that I am going to be completely transparent about. I have dreaded writing this because, well, I am embarrassed. I guess you could call this portion of my life my "ho era." Friends and family will

read this and form opinions, and I am sure they will be unsavory. But once again, I am a damn grown-up, and this is my story, and if I help someone else, writing it will be worth it.

In the fall of 2020, just three months after becoming a widow, I decided to sign up for online dating. Was I ready? Absolutely not, but I was in need of attention and validation outside of being told I was a good widow. I had not dated since 2008 and had never done the online thing. It was so overwhelming—I felt like fresh meat. The number of unsolicited dick pictures was atrocious; I thought that was a joke, but turns out it's real. I did meet one person; we started out by messaging back and forth, then speaking on the phone. We had sex a few times, but in the end, he wasn't what I was looking for. I knew what I wanted and what I deserved.

A couple of months later, I reconnected with someone via social media that I had dated over sixteen years before. Even though he was halfway across the country, our ability to connect and talk for hours about everything was refreshing. Fast-forward two months: he came for what was supposed to be a five-day visit. In the moment our connection felt undeniable; in hindsight, the familiarity was comforting. This five-day visit turned into him meeting my son and staying for three weeks. A couple of months later, he joined me for my friend's wedding in Maui, where we enjoyed a blissful week with each other. Nine weeks later, I then made the biggest change of my life, selling most of my belongings and moving 2,500 miles to South Carolina to make a better life for myself and my son. He was making the 1,200-mile trip from where he lived to help me settle in. I was so excited to have time with him in my new home.

Call it intuition if you will, but once I got here, somehow, I knew that he and I weren't going to work. If you have followed my story, you know one of my biggest flaws in my marriage was my inability to communicate my needs. News flash: still terrible at it, but I was going to give it a whirl. I probably should have been black and white about it, but I guess you can say I like to dance around the gray area. Instead of coming out point blank and saying exactly what I wanted, I treated our conversation like a first date or interview...
Me: "What are your five-year plans?"
Him: "Haven't really thought that far ahead."
Me: "Really? Okay, how about six months?"
Him: "Decide where I want to buy property and build my Airbnb business. What about you?"
Me: "Get Cash settled in football and school, start teaching again in September, probably start doing hair behind the chair in November, and have an amazing holiday season in our new home."

The feelings just weren't there. I didn't feel like his vision on life, his personality, and his demeanor aligned with what I really wanted and needed. The saddest part was I couldn't even come out and say it. The next morning, he packed his truck and left. We have not spoken since.

It felt like I'd lost Greg all over again, but really it just sank in that I'd never actually processed my loss; I'd found things to fill the space. It was time to focus on myself. Learn how to love myself, take the time to figure out exactly what I wanted in all aspects of my life. So that's what I did. I continued with my counseling sessions, journaled, and did things that made me happy. I started hiking again, taking Cash fishing, doing crafts projects, and I learned how to repair and refinish furniture. I found joy within myself.

Nine months later I started doing some dating, but nothing that was growing into anything serious. Once again, starting over is not an easy process. People have more baggage and trauma that didn't exist when I was dating in my early twenties, but finding a partner who is worth it is the key.

I was out for drinks with my friend Logan, updating her on someone I had been seeing, though I knew it wasn't going anywhere, and she instructed me to turn to my left and meet her friend Shelby.

There sat a handsome, bearded man with the kindest eyes. We closed the bar down, and I invited him to my house. He made sure I knew that nothing would be happening…It was refreshing, and we stayed up until almost 5:00 a.m. just talking. Our first date was later that afternoon. First, he bought me a helmet so I could ride on his motorcycle, and then he treated me to lunch and an afternoon at Top Golf, where the conversation didn't stop. I was giddy like a schoolgirl telling my friends about the date later that evening. They encouraged me to invite him over for drinks and cornhole, so I did, and they all approved. In fact, one said I would be stupid not to pursue him. We became inseparable.

We were together just over a week before my previously planned two-week vacation. It gave us the opportunity to connect on an emotional level before anything ever got physical. I was actually nervous when it came time for that special moment, and special it was. I feel guilty saying this, but it's true: I don't think I have ever connected more with a man on a physical level. It's not that Greg and I never connected physically—we did—

but somewhere along the way, sex became a mundane chore. Shelby and I were so in tune emotionally that when it came to the physicality of our relationship, it was easy.

We slid right into life together. He was pretty much living with us, doing my honey-do list, watching my son when I had to work evening shifts, showing up to football practices and games. It truly felt like he chose us, and we chose him…then he started pushing me away. At first, I thought I was going crazy and possibly imagining it. You should know that at this time my thyroid meds had to be changed and I wasn't feeling my best, so I waited to say something. It finally caught up with me, and I ended up crying at dinner, asking why he was pushing me away, but we had been together for eleven months, and he was making me feel insecure about our relationship.

A week later I ended things. I had to put myself first, even if it left a gaping hole in my heart. It was not easy, but standing up for my needs was important. I knew that if I continued, it would be a relationship full of resentment, and that was not healthy.

So I started working on myself again. Got back into therapy, focused on my journaling, and continued to write this very book. It gave me a lot of opportunities for introspection. I didn't realize I had naturally slipped into being a wife; since I had spent twelve years in that role, it was natural, but I needed to be a girlfriend. We both needed to learn about each other and our individual love languages and continue to have hobbies outside our relationship. I then realized that while I was expressive of my needs, he was right: I wasn't listening to his needs. I didn't allow him to take care of me in the way he needed to so that he felt that he was a supportive, validating partner. I started to ponder: If there had been better communication on both ends, could it have worked?

Three weeks after our breakup, he called to come pick up a fishing pole that was still at my house. We had just gotten home from football practice, I had put dinner in the oven, and my son was getting into the shower. As soon as Cash heard Shelby's voice, he put his dirty clothes back on and ran out of the bathroom, so excited to see him. Within minutes he invited him to stay for dinner. Shelby and I, both stunned, looked at each other, and I told him, "We have plenty, and you are more than welcome to stay," and he did.

While Cash was in the shower, Shelby joined me in the kitchen as I finished cooking, and we caught up on the past few weeks. Then he said to me, "I thought this would be more awkward," to which I replied, "What about us has ever felt awkward? The only time things felt off was when you pushed me away." He then said, "You're right," and we hugged. After Cash went to bed, we spent hours on the porch talking and ultimately decided we didn't want to live without each other. Our connection was too easy to ignore. Every relationship will have struggles—you just have to pick who you want to struggle with—and we have chosen each other.

Those three weeks of living in the lonely made my inner voice so loud I had no choice but to listen to what it was saying. The emotions I struggled with almost made me feel like I'd lost Greg all over again. I was reminded how important it is not to lose yourself in a relationship. Take time out of your day to spend with yourself; it doesn't have to be a lot. Even if it's just ten or fifteen minutes, take the time. Sit in silence, listen to positive affirmations, journal, sing, draw—do something for yourself. You have to remember to take care of your needs and not just the needs of those around you.

Most importantly, remember that a journey of grief is never done. You can momentarily fill that void with something else, but if you don't continue to do the necessary inner work, you can lose everything you've been working for, and that's something you'll regret.

Chapter 7
PARENTING SOLO

Parenting solo is daunting. I could not tell you the number of times I have cursed my husband up one side and down the other for leaving me in this position. Many times, I have said to myself, No one prepared me to do this alone. But truth be told, I was prepared. Now, I am not diminishing Greg's role as a father, but my role as a mother didn't change much after his death, because I was already doing a lot of the work myself. The hardest part is feeling like I am facing hard things alone…

    The first time I had to take my son to the emergency room was when he was ten years old. I know—how the hell did we manage to make it to ten? Your guess is as good as mine. His first time on a dirt bike was at three years old. He started football at six years old, weighing forty-two pounds, and rode to practice in a five-point harness car seat. Call it dumb luck, I guess.

We had been living in South Carolina for eight months, and I suspected he had broken his arm. It was the first time I had stepped foot into an ER since the fateful day of Greg's death—nothing like facing two fears at once. They got us into a room quickly and took Cash in for X-rays, and shortly afterward the doctor came back with news that he had fractured his arm. I lost it, broke down sobbing. The doctor started consoling me, telling me it's not uncommon for a child to break his arm. I responded with "I can handle a broken arm; I am crying in relief. I guess I didn't know how overwhelmed I was walking in these doors. I was afraid to walk out of them alone again." I was starting to own my story.

Shortly after Cash broke his arm, another incident occurred that drove home just how hard solo parenting is. My son had always begged to ride the bus home from school, and when he was in fifth grade, I started letting him. It was an easy transition, and I loved not having to deal with the pick-up line. Then all of a sudden, he was waking up with night terrors, dreaded going to school, and was super clingy. He didn't tell me at first, but he was being bullied. The saddest part is that he was being bullied for his dad being dead. I tried to encourage him to ignore it, telling him that the bully was probably having problems at home, that maybe he just needed to be understanding.

One afternoon he'd had enough, and he walked into the house with tears in his eyes. He said, "Mom, I know you said I could never hit a girl, but you didn't say I couldn't hit a girl with a water bottle."

I couldn't argue with that. I just hugged him and asked him what had happened. Once again, she had made fun of him for his dad being dead, and not one of his friends on the bus had stood up for him. It all started to make sense: in all his night terrors, he was trying to save his dad, he did not feel comfortable going to school, and I was his safe person. Cash had started therapy within weeks of his father's passing but had since graduated and hadn't seen a therapist in over a year.

The very next day, I sought out help. I first emailed (refraining from writing every profane word I wanted to use in this message) and then met in person with his teacher, his vice principal, the school counselor, and later another therapist. Advocating for my child.

I constantly catch myself trying to face every mountain that comes my way on my own. Writing this chapter has helped me realize that even though I often feel alone, I am not. I am supported, and those around me are willing to offer help; I just need to swallow my pride and ask for it. Asking for help is not a sign of weakness; it is a sign of strength. I was recently reminded that it makes me feel good to help others when they need it, so asking someone else for help is just me returning the favor and allowing another person the opportunity to feel good.

Chapter 8
VISITING THE PAST

Some say I ran away from the situation when I moved my son and myself across the country, and I guess in a sense I did. I like to think I was running to the life I was looking to build. I knew that I could not grow into the person I needed to be while living in the same house and the same city, around the same things, in a life that no longer existed for me. So instead of replaying the parts of my life that held me in my grief, I chose to move forward. I chose to create a life where I wasn't feeling smothered by the loss, a life where I wasn't just surviving, one where I could breathe.

My first visit back to California after I moved was in November for Thanksgiving. I had been in South Carolina only five months, but it was on that trip that I realized for myself that California was no longer home. I worked a few days in my old salon there, and even that wasn't feeling familiar anymore. It took me a couple of months to accept the fact, but I knew it was time to completely let that part of my life go.

In February 2022, I visited again, and I sold the salon. I knew it was no longer my dream, and it deserved someone who could give it the time, energy, and love a business needs. A wise person (yes, Eileen, it was you) once told me, "When you hold on to something too long, it becomes heavy."

The salon was part of my past and a life that no longer served me. Holding on to it was weighing me down and holding me back from what the future had in store. You see, the last big project Greg and I had done together was the salon. We painted; installed the mirrors, shelving, and shampoo bowls; and hung decor. We even put in a sprinkler system, because I told him there was no way our marriage was going to make it through the summer if I had to hand water the grass. I was standing in that very building when my phone rang, shattering my whole world and turning my life upside down. The time had come to set that memory down, and I did so by handing over the keys to the new owner.

One year and eight months. That was how long I'd stayed away from California after selling the salon, and quite honestly, it probably would have been longer, but my best friend's daughter was getting married, and she was quite insistent that I attend, so I did. Originally it was going to be my son, Cash; my boyfriend, Shelby; and me making this trip, but at the last minute, because of issues at work, Shelby had to stay home. At first, I was devastated. I was ready for him to meet my friends and family in California, but I knew there had to be a reason he couldn't come, and the universe was up to something.

I flew in on Wednesday night, and first thing Thursday morning, I had a hair appointment. I walked into the salon expecting to be hit with a wave of emotions, but I wasn't. Everything was different. The mirror where I'd seen the panic in my face when I heard the words "Greg is having a heart attack" had been replaced. The station where I threw my tools, which quickly fell to the floor, was not the same. New products decorated the shelves, the walls were painted a different color, and new decor adorned every corner. What had once been my home away from home no longer represented me. It was the same corner lot, the same name, and the same building where my life had changed three years, three months, and eighteen days prior, but the change no longer felt grievous.

The next day I found myself childless for a few hours and decided to go to the mall to do some much-needed bra shopping. If you have ever been bra shopping for yourself or with someone, you know it is one of the most cumbersome shopping experiences. I loathe trying bras on. Halfway through what felt like one hundred bras (realistically ten), I was sweaty, cranky, and looking for any excuse to be done. So I came up with a grand plan: if I could find a couple of bras that I was happy with, I could go look for a new outfit for the wedding, even though we all know I already had five options I had packed in my suitcase. It felt like an eternity of searching for and trying on bras, but I was successful, so now the shopping fun could begin. Or so I thought. The funny thing about grief is you have no idea when the waves are going to ebb and flow, and they seem to hit at the most inopportune times.

There I was, walking through the dress department of one of the main anchor stores, and it hit me. The last time I was in this very spot was when I was searching for a dress to wear to Greg's memorial. As the weight of the memory grew heavier, silent tears started streaming down my face. People gazed at me with concern in their eyes; it was the same expression I had dreaded in the months following his death. I had to step outside to catch my breath because I knew the sobs would soon follow.

Throughout this journey of grief, I have discovered that suppressing your emotions only prolongs the ache. So I sobbed. Outside the mall. The same mall where we would take Cash to have his Santa picture taken. The same store where Cash decided to play hide-and-seek in a clothing rack while the three of us were Christmas shopping together, sending me into an absolute frenzy. The same building where I purchased Greg's tie for our wedding. I had no intention to revisit old memories; I had planned only to shop for bras. Determined not to let this building get the best of me, I gathered my emotions, stepped back inside, and indulged in a new lipstick, because lipstick always fits.

The universe is always sending me gentle reminders to live in the present. Sometimes you never know the true value of a moment until it becomes a memory.

Cash and I were so lucky to spend the rest of Friday, Saturday, and Sunday surrounded by friends and family eager to hear about our new life. Quite honestly, I almost felt like we were bragging. While there are times I desperately miss the relationships we have on the West Coast, nothing compares to the relationship Cash and I have developed through learning to navigate this world without Greg in it.

On Monday morning Cash asked if we could go to his favorite doughnut shop and drive by our old house on the way to see friends, and we did. I drove the same route I did on that dreadful day of June 17, 2020. I inhaled a deep breath at the same stop sign where I'd sent my mom the 911 text message and then made the left-hand turn onto Treebine. It didn't hurt. The house was a different color, there was a new mailbox, and the tree in the front yard was taller. It was no longer our home.

As we drove away, the Rival Sons song "Jordan" came on, and Cash said, "See, Mom, Dad's still with us!" Cash and Greg saw Rival Sons in early 2019, and while it wasn't the first concert Cash had ever been to, it was the most memorable. He clung to the story behind the song, and just a few months later, Cash sang it to his grandfather (Greg's dad) in the hospital, and there wasn't a dry eye in the room. The next morning, Greg's dad passed. I never doubt that Greg is with us, and the signs he sends are always comforting.

In the car we continued driving. On the overpass that had become the setting where I'd shared the heartbreaking news of Greg's death with my sister, Cash said, "Thank you, Mom."

"For what?" I replied.

"For moving us to South Carolina. Everyone in our family that stayed here stayed sad. They are still the same. We are happy, we are stronger, and I love our life."

A tear of joy—maybe it was happiness or even accomplishment; hell, I would even say pride—slid down my cheek. "You're welcome, Puppy; I love our life too."

Some say I ran away...call it whatever you want, but that "Thank you, Mom" on that overpass was worth it.

Chapter 9
THE BEST THING THAT HAPPENED TO ME

Yes, I did say that becoming a widow at the age of thirty-four was the best thing that has ever happened to me. Just a friendly reminder: if you don't like what I have to say, read elsewhere.

I promise it doesn't come from a mean place; I loved and still very much love my late husband. If he were alive today, there is no doubt in my mind we would still be married. We were a team; he was my best friend, the most amazing father I have ever known, and a friend that everyone could count on. His jokes were endless, as were his hobbies, and I always pictured doing life with him.

What I gained the day my husband earned his wings was perspective. At the end of the day, it doesn't matter what you own or what you do for a living. The one question you should ponder answering is this: What is most important? When I asked myself this question, I realized how many moments in life I had sacrificed for the job and the bottom dollar. I had given up watching my child's football games, fishing on the boat, witnessing the first time my child rode a dirt bike, and attending countless birthday parties and dinners, all because I "had to work."

Our first year in South Carolina, I was able to take a break and finally find balance between work and family. Putting my faith in God and trust in my intuition, I knew it was time to make a big life change. For an entire year, I got to live at the other end of the scale. If you had told me a few years ago that I would make the choice not to work for six months and then decide I really needed a year to spend the time focusing on my child and myself, I would have placed a million-dollar bet against it…but I did it…and I loved it, because it was during this time that I found what's most important. Our happiness.

Chapter 10
OTHER SHIT CAN WAIT

I am not writing this chapter for widows or widowers who are just starting their journeys but for the person who is helping someone navigate the burden of this story. Or if I am being completely honest, it's probably a quick elbow in the rib cage to my future self.

I have had numerous women tell me that if their spouses passed away, they would be fine on their own and could never see themselves in another relationship. Just so you know, it takes everything I have not to throat punch you and burst into tears all at the same time. And the craziest part about it all is that I, too, once felt the same way. Trust me when I say this now: you'll miss it when it's gone.

Let me get sappy for a moment. You know the song by Diamond Rio called "One More Day"?

One more day, one more time

One more sunset, maybe I'd be satisfied
But then again, I know what it would do.
Leave me wishing still for one more day with you.

 I cannot tell you how many moments I have thought about what I would do if I had one more day with Greg. What would I cook for him? Would I make his favorite dessert or mine? Would I worry about whether or not the honey-do list was done, or would we spend the day doing fun activities? Would I want the day alone with him or with all our family? Until you are in this position, you have no idea what losing your spouse truly feels like, and it is no easy feat. So my advice to you all and to myself in the future is this: make that meal, eat that dessert, do those fun activities, and spend time together. The other shit can wait.

Setting It Down

After only an hour of sleep, my intuition told me to get the hell up and write. All I kept hearing in my mind was "The book isn't going to write itself." As I glanced at the phone to check the time, it struck me. It was currently 6:53 a.m. on the date that would have marked our eighth wedding anniversary and over fifteen years together.

It has been a long road. As I write this, I am three years, five months, and eleven days into widowhood and a little over two years into writing this book. Some people have asked why it has taken so long to finish; the truth is, I knew there was more that the book needed. There were things I had not experienced until the last couple of months, and they were milestones in my healing process. I don't think the book would have been complete without the last few chapters. Now I can sit here reflecting on how far I have come since becoming a widow, and I am incredibly proud. I have become the mother that I have always dreamed of being, but most importantly I have become a better person for myself.

The journey hasn't been easy, and there have been many times I felt like I was failing. Not today. Today I am ready to set down my "widow armor." I will always have my badge of widowhood, but today it no longer defines me as a person. Today I am Kenna, a more patient, strong, smart, determined, loving, and caring individual. A mother, sister, daughter, aunt, cousin, niece, granddaughter, friend, and girlfriend. I am a football mom, hair artist, bartender, and social media guru. There is not one word that defines where I am in my life, and the possibilities are endless.

It's a little bittersweet that the date we vowed to spend the rest of our lives together is the day I intuitively chose to finish writing this book. I am choosing to pass along the habits I embraced to survive in hopes they may help other young widows or widowers. As for me, it's time to thrive…as Kenna.

www.ingramcontent.com/pod-product-compliance
Lightning Source LLC
LaVergne TN
LVHW051924060526
838201LV00062B/4679